CONTENTS

S0-ASK-815

INTRODUCTION

Drying flowers is something we try to do to preserve the beauty of the summer through the winter months. What many of us also try to do at some time in our lives is to press an individual flower or leaf because we want to invest it with a special memory. The wonderful thing about pressing, rather than just drying flowers, is that they tend to hold their colours better. I often find a flower or leaf fluttering out from a book that I had taken on holiday years before, and remember when it was that I picked that particular flower. Hanging on the wall at home, I have a small collage of all things American, which is a mixture of printed labels and orange and red maple leaves from a holiday in New England.

In this book we have taken the idea of saving flowers a step further; not only do we have ideas for displaying those special flowers full of memories, we have also created over 20 fantastic projects for you to make for your home using pressed flowers. Don't worry about whether or not you have the right equipment, we show you how to make your own flower press and provide full step-by-step instructions for each project. There are also comprehensive materials, equipment and techniques sections at the back of the book, which means that you can't go far wrong.

So next time you are sitting in your own garden, or on holiday abroad, and pick a flower and press it in the pages of your book, don't just use it as a bookmark, think about where you could use it in your home.

Deborah Barker

WOODLAND CANDLES

Cool green leaves and ferns are ideal partners for the waxy texture of neutral-coloured candles.
Decide how you wish the finished design to look, then fix the leaves in place with melted wax.

YOU WILL NEED
double boiler or saucepan and heatproof bowl
cheese grater
neutral-coloured candle ends
pressed green leaves or ferns
square or round, thick neutral-coloured candles
medium-sized artist's paintbrush

1 Prepare boiling water in a double boiler or a bowl of water over a saucepan. Grate the candle ends into the bowl so that the wax melts.

Above: You can decorate candles of all shapes and sizes with leaves and flowers.

2 Arrange pressed leaves or ferns around the sides of a large candle. Gently stick them in place, using the melted wax and a paintbrush. Seal with a thin layer of melted wax.

WAXED FLOWER GIFT BAGS

These beautifully constructed bags and matching gift tags are cleverly made of traditional waxed sandwich wrapping paper, available from supermarkets.

YOU WILL NEED
ruler
waxed sandwich wrapping paper
adhesive tape
tweezers
pressed verbena and *Achillea mollis* flowers
iron
scissors
natural (garden) raffia
double-sided tape
coloured handmade paper
white paper
spray adhesive
hole punch

1 Enlarge the template at the back of the book to the size required on a photocopier. Tear a piece of waxed sandwich paper to fit over your template and tape it on top, with the shiny side facing up.

2 Using tweezers, arrange the verbena flowers in a diamond grid pattern on the front and back of the bag shape. The bottom of each flower should face towards the centre base line.

3 Select tiny flowers from the *Achillea mollis* and place them between the verbena flowers. Carefully lay a second piece of waxed paper on top, shiny side down.

4 Using a cool iron, gently press the waxed paper so that the petals are fixed. Allow to cool. Cut out the waxed paper to the size of your template.

5 With the waxed paper face down on top of the template, fold down the top hems. Fold the bag in half crossways and open out.

6 Fold the sides in along the inside line, then back along the outer line. Open out the last fold. Crease along the lines to either side of the central fold.

7 Lift the side fold and turn at 45 degrees to make a diagonal crease. Match the crease lines as shown. Open out, crease the other end and repeat on the other side.

8 Fold up the bag so that two neat triangular folds the width of the base of the bag are created on the inside. Tuck one side panel into the other along the top edge.

9 Snip two small triangles on the front and back panels, next to the inside folds. Make a plaited raffia handle and attach under the rim with double-sided tape.

▶

10 To make the gift tag, fold a 7.5 x 15 cm/ 3 x 6 in square of coloured handmade paper in half. Mark a window at one end in pencil, then cut out along the drawn lines.

11 Sandwich four petals between two layers of waxed paper, and insert into the window on the reverse side. Cut a piece of white paper to stick on top, using spray adhesive.

12 Fold the gift tag in half and punch a hole in one top corner. Thread a loop of raffia though the hole and pull the ends through the loop.

Above: You could make an attractive greetings card using the same technique as for the gift tag.

FLOWER PAPER

*Decorate your own handmade paper with coloured threads and petals then add the name
of the flower you have used in printed letters.*

YOU WILL NEED
15 sheets of plain white typing paper
bowl
liquidizer or hand-held blender
scissors
scraps of coloured cotton fabric
staple gun
40 cm/16 in square of tulle
2 wooden frames, each 18 cm/7 in square
shallow plastic tray
wooden spoon
2 plastic or marble pastry boards
pressed flower petals
kitchen towels
heavy weight
page of text from old book
PVA (white) glue and fine paintbrush

1 Tear the paper into pieces approximately
2.5 cm/1 in square. Place them in a bowl, cover
with cold water and leave to soak overnight.

2 Put a handful of damp paper
in the liquidizer or blender,
and add enough water to bring the
level up to two-thirds full. Process
for 15–20 seconds to break down
the fibres. Pour the paper pulp
into a bowl and set aside.

3 Cut the coloured fabric into
small pieces. Place in the
liquidizer or blender and cover
with water. Process the fabric
until it has separated into individual threads.

4 To make the mould, staple
the tulle to one of the
wooden frames at the centre of
each side then staple each side,
maintaining an even tension.
Trim the surplus fabric.

▶

5 Pour the paper pulp into a shallow tray and fill with water to within 5 cm/2 in of the top. Add the liquidized fabric and stir thoroughly.

6 Hold the mould with the tulle side upwards then place the second frame (the deckle) on top. Dip the two into the pulp and hold them level under the surface.

7 Lift the mould and deckle out of the pulp. Keeping them level, agitate them gently until most of the water has drained away.

8 Remove the deckle and place the mould on a plastic or marble board. Arrange the pressed petals on the layer of damp pulp.

9 Lay a kitchen towel on the board. Carefully invert the mould on to the towel and press it down, then lift it carefully so that the pulp remains on the towel. Place another kitchen towel on top of the pulp layer. Repeat with the rest of the pulp. Place a second board over the final sheet of pulp and put a heavy weight on top. Leave to dry overnight.

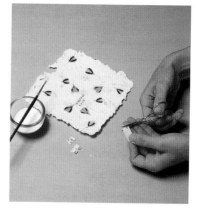

10 Cut out letters from the printed text to spell out the Latin name of the pressed flowers. Glue on to the paper, using a fine brush.

LILY-PETAL LANTERNS

These simply made paper lanterns are decorated with dramatic partially cut-out lily petals.

Place each lantern over a small glass jar containing a nightlight (tealight).

YOU WILL NEED
pencil
scissors
large sheets of textured handmade paper
hole punch
pressed lily petals
PVA (white) glue
fine artist's paintbrush
kitchen sponge
cutting mat
craft knife
string
double-sided tape
small glass jars
nightlights (tealights)

1 Enlarge the template at the back of the book to the desired size on a photocopier, and cut out. For each lantern, draw round the template on to handmade paper. Lightly mark the overlap and hole positions.

2 Use the scissors to cut out the lantern shape.

3 Punch two holes where marked, using a hole punch.

4 Apply PVA (white) glue to the back of each lily petal with a fine paintbrush.

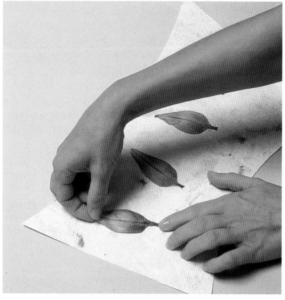

5 Carefully place about four lily petals on to the paper lantern.

6 Press each petal gently in place with a slightly damp sponge to make sure the edges are firmly glued to the paper.

7 Place the lantern on a cutting mat. Carefully cut most of the way round each petal with a craft knife to form a little flap.

8 Cut a piece of string about 45 cm/18 in long. Thread it through the two small holes so that both ends emerge on the decorated side of the lantern.

9 Bend the lantern round to form a cylinder, overlapping the edges where indicated. Secure with small pieces of double-sided tape. Tie the ends of string together with a double knot.

LAVENDER SACHET

Shot organdie and delicate pressed flowers make a lovely container for sweet-scented lavender.
If tubular ribbon is difficult to find, you can make your own using transparent fabric.

YOU WILL NEED
scissors
shot organdie in three colours
sewing machine
matching sewing threads
iron
metallic sewing thread
dressmaker's pins
pressed flowers in colours to complement the organdie
(e.g. azaleas, verbenas)
embroidered organdie for the backing fabric
transparent tubular ribbon
dried lavender

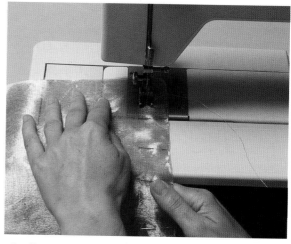

1 Cut two strips 20 x 30 cm/8 x 12 in and one strip 25 x 30 cm/10 x 12 in from three different colours of shot organdie. The widest strip will be the cuff of the bag. Machine stitch the strips together, leaving a seam allowance of 2 cm/³/₄ in.

2 Press the seams open, using a cool iron. Zigzag stitch on the right side, using metallic thread.

3 Cut several small rectangular patches from all three colours of organdie. Using a pin, gently fray around all four sides of each patch.

4 Place a patch on the right side of the prepared fabric and pin one side to secure. Place one or more pressed flowers under the patch then pin the other three sides.

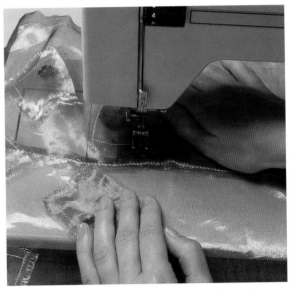

5 Machine stitch around the edges of the patch, using straight stitch and metallic thread. Repeat with the rest of the patches.

6 Cut a piece of embroidered organdie to the same size as the stiched-together strips of flower-decorated organdie. Place the two wrong sides together and machine along three sides.

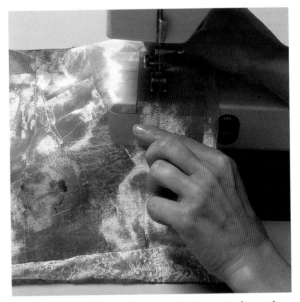

7 Fold down the cuff strip and zigzag stitch on the right side. Turn the bag right side out.

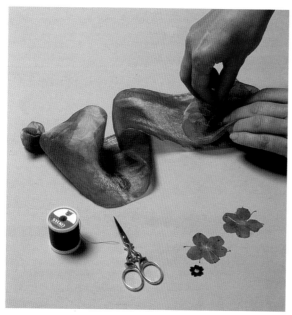

8 Tie one end of the transparent tubular ribbon
  securely with matching sewing thread, then pour
in some pressed flowers. Disperse the flowers evenly,
and tie the other end tightly with thread.

9 Fill the finished bag with dried lavender. Tie the
  open end of the bag with the flower-filled ribbon.

GRASS-DECORATED VASE

*Pressed grasses provide a simple but elegant decoration on this handmade papier-mâché vase,
which is neatly constructed around two card (cardboard) cones.*

YOU WILL NEED
tracing paper
pencil
thin card (cardboard)
thick card (cardboard)
strong scissors
masking tape
small scissors
newspaper
wallpaper paste and brush
medium-grade sandpaper
cream emulsion (latex) paint
small decorator's paintbrush
PVA (white) glue
fine artist's paintbrush
pressed grasses
kitchen sponge
clear acrylic spray

1 Enlarge the templates at the back of the book to
the size required on a photocopier. Trace the
main shapes on to thin card (cardboard), and the base
on to thick card. Cut out all the shapes.

2 Take the smaller upper shape and bend into a
cone. Secure the overlap with masking tape.

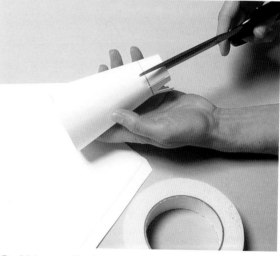

3 Using small scissors, snip into the cone where
marked to make small tabs.

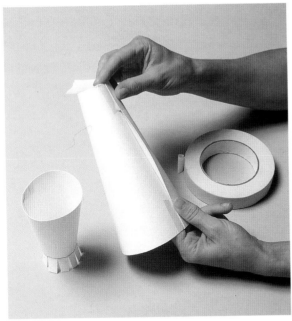

4 Take the larger lower shape and bend into another cone, securing the overlap with masking tape as before.

5 Insert the tabs of the upper cone into the neck of the lower cone to make the vase shape.

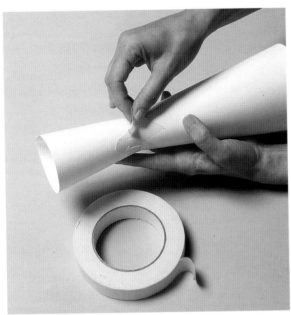

6 Hold the two cones together and secure them with a strip of masking tape.

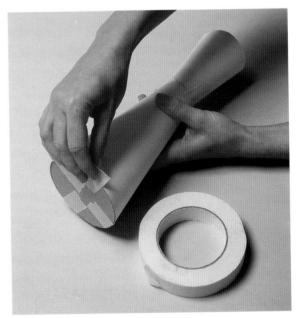

7 Turn the vase upside down and insert the base. Secure it firmly with tabs of masking tape.

8 Tear strips of newspaper about 2.5 cm/1 in wide. Paste each strip in turn with wallpaper paste and place on to the vase until it is completely covered. Wrap the strips around and over the top edge, making sure they are firmly stuck down on the inside. Apply about eight layers then leave to dry.

9 When the papier-mâché is completely dry, smooth the surface with sandpaper.

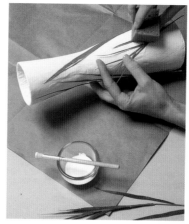

10 Apply two or three coats of cream emulsion (latex) paint, allowing each coat to dry before applying the next. Leave to dry.

11 Using a fine paintbrush, apply PVA (white) glue to the pressed grasses then position them on the side of the vase using a sponge. Leave to dry.

12 Apply two coats of clear acrylic spray, allowing time to dry between each coat.

NATURE NOTEBOOK

Use this rustic album to display your collection of pressed flowers and leaves. Fill the pages before assembling the album, or leave them blank to be filled in later.

YOU WILL NEED
utility knife, cutting mat and metal ruler
heavier-weight handmade paper for the cover
silicone paper, or other smooth-textured paper
spoon
fine Japanese tissue paper or other semi-transparent paper
various handmade and plant papers for the pages
glue stick
selection of pressed flowers to decorate the cover
fine artist's paintbrush
PVA (white) glue
large bulldog clip
pencil
hole punch or wad punch
hammer
large-eyed darning needle
natural (garden) raffia
handmade string, fine twine or coarse linen thread

1 Cut a piece of handmade paper for the cover twice as long as the desired page size. Fold in half along the short edge then smooth the crease under a protective sheet of silicone paper or other smooth-textured paper. Tear the two short edges to give a natural effect.

2 Cut sheets of tissue paper to the same size as the desired page size. Cut or tear the pages out of an interesting selection of handmade and plant papers.

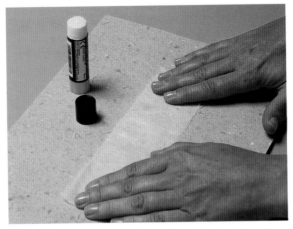

3 Tear a strip of tissue paper into a rectangle and glue to the front of the cover with a glue stick.

▶

4 Arrange the pressed flowers on the tissue paper. Using a fine paintbrush, glue them down individually with a small dab of PVA (white) glue in the centre of each flower. Leave to dry, then carefully apply tiny dabs of glue on the petals to stop them from lifting.

5 Using PVA glue and a fine paintbrush, decorate the pages with pressed flowers. Alternatively, leave the pages blank to be filled in later.

6 Assemble the pages with a sheet of tissue paper between each one to protect the flowers. Hold in place with a bulldog clip. Mark the position of holes for stitching, then pierce with a punch and hammer. Pierce holes in both sides of the cover to match.

7 Using the darning needle, thread short lengths of raffia and string together through the first two holes at the top and bottom and knot individually. Thread the needle again with a longer length of raffia only, and back stitch through the remaining holes. Repeat with the string. Tie the ends neatly at the back of the notebook and trim off the ends.

SUMMER GARDEN LAMP

Collect a colourful mixture of flowers and leaves for this lovely translucent lamp, to create the effect of a traditional flower border. The bamboo structure is very sturdy but always place it on a flat surface.

YOU WILL NEED
sharp knife
green bamboo cane
scissors
natural (garden) raffia
thin card (cardboard)
PVA (white) glue
double-sided tape
abaca tissue
spray adhesive
pressed flowers and leaves
tweezers
clear acrylic spray
fire-retardant spray
nightlight (tealight)

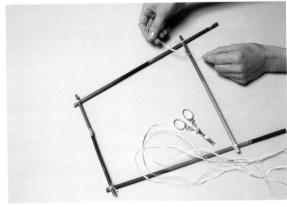

1 Cut three pieces of bamboo 38 cm/15 in, 28 cm/11 in and 20 cm/8 in. Lay the two longer pieces vertically and tie the short piece across the top, using raffia. Tie an extra piece to fit across 7.5 cm/ 3 in from the bottom of the longer piece.

2 Add more pieces of bamboo cane as shown to create a three-dimensional triangular structure,. Tied together with raffia. Make sure the bottom triangle is parallel to the worksurface.

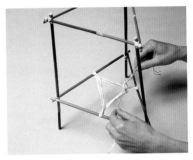

3 Wrap a length of raffia around the bottom triangle to make a support for a nightlight (tealight). Tie the ends securely. Cut a triangle of card (cardboard) the same size and glue on top.

4 Stick double-sided tape along the inside of the bamboo frame. Cut a piece of abaca tissue to size and stick in position on one side of the lamp. Cut across the corners to expose the raffia and trim to 1 cm/ ¹/₂ in. Fold the excess to the inside. ▶

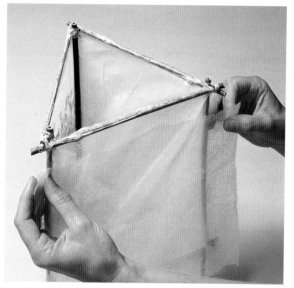

5 Build up several graduated layers of abaca tissue on the sides of the lamp, using spray adhesive to secure them in place. Tear neatly down each side against the edge of the bamboo cane, and turn the top and bottom edges to the inside.

6 Spray the abaca tissue with two coats of adhesive, then begin to arrange the more delicate flowers and leaves near the top of the lamp, using tweezers.

7 Work down the lamp, using progressively larger flowers and leaves. Mix the colours and shapes to create a summer border effect.

8 Spray the finished lamp with several coats of clear acrylic spray followed by a coat of fire-retardant spray. Leave to dry. To use, light a nightlight (tealight) and lift carefully on to the card platform from below.

FRAMED FLOWER HEAD

A beautiful scabious flower deserves to be displayed on the wall in a small colour-washed frame.

Adjust the paint colours to complement other flowers.

YOU WILL NEED
pencil
ruler
80 cm/32 in length of softwood,
(7.5 cm/3 in wide and
2 cm/³/₄ in thick)
mitre block
saw
wood glue
staple gun
white card (cardboard)
craft knife
wine cork
PVA (white) glue
fine artist's paintbrush
small decorator's paintbrush
white emulsion (latex) paint
acrylic paint in pale green
and dark blue
medium-sized artist's
paintbrush
pressed scabious flower head
double-sided tape

1 Mark the softwood into four equal lengths of 20 cm/8 in then mark a 45 degree angle at each end.

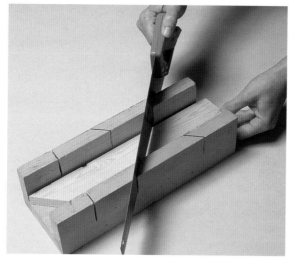

2 Place the wood in a mitre block and cut along the marked angles with a saw.

3 Glue the four pieces together with wood glue to make a square frame. Leave to dry.

4 Reinforce the glued joins on the reverse side, using a staple gun.

5 Cut a piece of white card (cardboard) the same size as the frame. Using a craft knife, cut a 1 cm/$^{1}/_{2}$ in piece of cork to support the flower head.

6 Glue the cork support to the centre of the card. This will act as a backing board.

7 Apply two coats of white emulsion (latex) paint to the front of the frame and the backing board, allowing each to dry before applying the next.

8 Take up a little pale green acrylic paint on a dry paintbrush and lightly brush over the front of the frame to leave a trace of paint on the surface.

9 Using an artist's paintbrush, colour the inside and outside edge of the frame with dark blue acrylic paint.

▶

10 Glue the scabious flower head to the cork support in the centre of the card.

11 Centre the frame over the backing board and hold in place with strips of double-sided tape.

PAPER BOWLS

*Place these enchanting bowls near a window or a lamp, so that the light shines through
the paper and illuminates the petals and leaves just below the surface.*

YOU WILL NEED
small bowl to use as a mould
plastic food wrap
spray furniture polish
handmade white Japanese mulberry paper
medium-sized artist's paintbrush
fabric stiffener
spoon
pressed rose, gerbera and chrysanthemum petals
pressed leaves
kitchen sponge
handmade yellow and green Japanese mulberry paper (optional)
clear acrylic spray

1 Turn the bowl upside down and cover with
plastic food wrap.

2 Spray the surface with furniture polish. (This
acts as a releasing agent when you remove the
finished bowl.)

3 Tear the mulberry paper into small, irregular
pieces. It is important to tear it rather than using
scissors as this gives a soft, uneven edge.

4 Using a paintbrush, apply a little fabric stiffener to the surface of the mould, then begin to build up the first layer of paper pieces. Brush the pieces flat.

5 Apply about four more layers, brushing each layer smooth.

6 Gently rub the back of a spoon over the surface to remove air bubbles, and ensure all the pieces are stuck firmly together.

7 Prepare the flower petals and leaves, then brush a little more fabric stiffener over the surface of the paper.

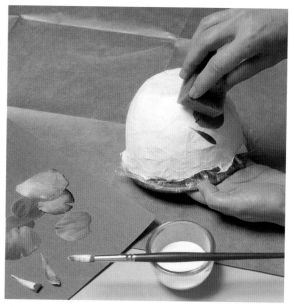

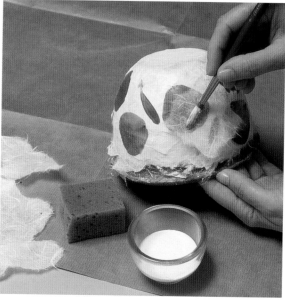

8 Arrange a few rose and gerbera petals on the bowl in a random pattern. To vary the design, add a few strips of coloured mulberry paper, some chrysanthemum petals or some leaves.

9 Apply a thin layer of paper to protect but not obscure the flower petals. Leave to dry completely.

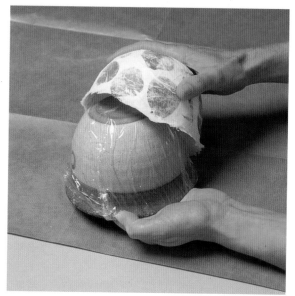

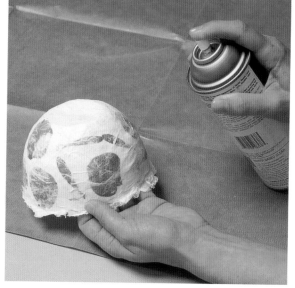

10 When completely dry, gently prise the paper bowl away from the mould.

11 Spray the inside and outside of the bowl with two layers of clear acrylic spray, allowing the bowl to dry between each layer.

DAISY CHAIN CLOCK

Make your own small clock, and tell the time with an enchanting circle of marguerites.
A hint of pale yellow paint echoes the colour of the flower centres.

YOU WILL NEED
pencil
ruler
piece of 3 mm/¹/₈ in thick MDF
(medium-density fibre board)
cutting mat
utility knife
metal ruler
plastic ruler
hacksaw
wooden quadrant
wood glue and brush

white emulsion (latex) paint
small decorator's paintbrush
wallpaper paste and brush
white tissue paper
pale yellow acrylic paint
PVA (white) glue and brush
pressed marguerites,
with stems
clear acrylic spray
drill
clock mechanism and hands

1 Mark two 15 cm/6 in squares, two
15 x 7.5 cm/6 x 3 in rectangles and one
7.5 x 15 cm/3 x 6 in rectangle on the piece of MDF
(medium-density fibre board).

2 Using a cutting mat, cut out the marked shapes
with a utility knife and metal ruler.

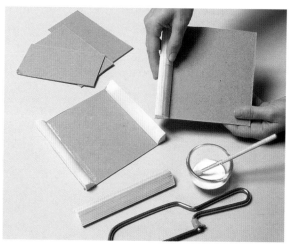

3 Cut four 15 cm/6 in lengths of wooden quadrant
and glue one to either side of the two MDF
squares, using wood glue.

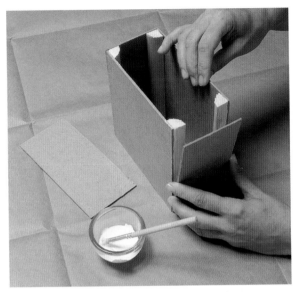

4 Glue the two smaller rectangles and the two squares together to make a box shape. Glue the remaining rectangle to the top.

5 Apply two coats of white emulsion (latex) paint, allowing each coat to dry before applying the next one.

6 Working on each side in turn, apply a thin coat of wallpaper paste, then lay on a piece of tissue paper. Gently wrinkle the tissue paper with your fingers and pat it to remove any air bubbles. Tear the tissue paper close to the edges of the clock base.

7 When the tissue paper is dry, take up a little pale yellow acrylic paint on a dry paintbrush and drag it lightly over the surface to leave just a trace of paint.

8 Apply a little PVA (white) glue to the back of each marguerite and place in a circle on the clock face to represent numerals. Glue a few marguerites on the sides and the top.

9 Apply two coats of clear acrylic spray, allowing each coat to dry before applying the next.

10 Drill a hole in the centre of the clock face just large enough for the shaft of the clock mechanism to pass through.

11 Insert the clock mechanism and attach the hands, following the manufacturer's instructions.

MONTBRETIA SCREEN

A small three-panel screen is an ideal way to make the most of long-stemmed flowers.
Repeat the same flower, or feature a different plant on each panel.

YOU WILL NEED
ruler
utility knife
fine green bamboo cane
glue gun
white linen thread
scissors
white cotton tulle
pressed montbretia flowers, with long stems

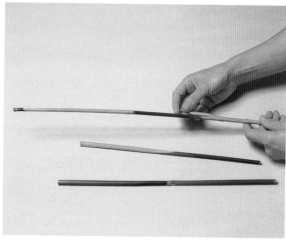

1 For each panel, cut two 18 cm/7 in and two
35 cm/14 in lengths of green bamboo cane. Strip
away the brown covering.

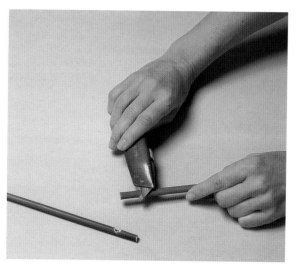

2 Cut a small notch 2.5 cm/1 in from the ends of
each piece of bamboo cane so that they will lie
flat when bound together.

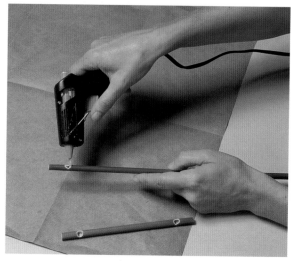

3 Matching the notches, glue the pieces together
with a glue gun to make a rectangular frame.

4 Bind the corners of the frame with linen thread to secure the joints.

5 Cut two 18 x 35 cm/7 x 14 in rectangles from the tulle.

6 Glue one of the tulle rectangles to one side of the bamboo frame.

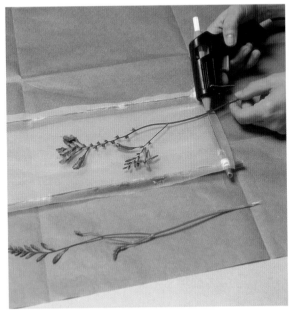

7 Glue the ends of the montbretia stems to one short side of the frame and arrange the montbretia attractively.

8 Glue the second tulle rectangle to the same side of the frame so that the montbretia is trapped between the two layers. Trim the raw edges of both pieces of tulle.

9 Make two more panels the same way. Cut four short lengths of bamboo cane and slot into the hollow ends of the bamboo cane on the bottom sides of each frame to join the panels together.

FLOWER-STUDDED BALLS

Larkspur flowers and rose petals cover these delightful decorations, which would make lovely gifts.
Make them in a range of sizes for an unusual display.

YOU WILL NEED
mould-making alginate powder
spoon
plastic container, slightly larger than the polystyrene ball
polystyrene ball
plaster of Paris powder
small mixing jug
knife
medium-grade sandpaper
PVA (white) glue and brush
fine artist's paintbrush
pressed larkspur flowers and rose petals
clear acrylic spray

1 Following the manufacturer's instructions, mix together some alginate powder and water in the plastic container.

2 Plunge the polystyrene ball halfway into the mixture. Hold it steady for a few minutes until the alginate begins to set.

3 When the alginate feels firm and rubbery, gently prise the ball away to leave a mould.

4 Mix some plaster of Paris powder with water in a small jug to a creamy consistency. Pour it into the mould and tap the sides gently to release air bubbles. ▶

5 Leave the plaster to set hard. Flex the mould slightly until the plaster shape pops out. Make another shape the same way

6 Mix a little plaster of Paris powder to a thick consistency. Using a knife, spread it on the flat side of one plaster shape. Press the other shape on top to form a complete ball. Leave to dry.

7 Sand the surface of the ball to smooth out any unevenness or rough edges.

8 Apply a coat of PVA (white) glue then begin to add the pressed larkspur flowers and rose petals, using a fine paintbrush.

9 Place the flowers and petals close together to cover the entire surface. Leave to dry.

10 Apply two or three coats of clear acrylic spray, allowing each coat to dry before applying the next.

CHECKERBOARD TRAY

Stencil a wooden tray with a grid of squares then decorate each square with pansy flowers and sunny yellow chrysanthemum petals.

YOU WILL NEED
wooden tray
emulsion (latex) paint in pale blue, yellow and white
medium decorator's paintbrush
ruler
soft pencil
thin paper
stencil acetate
craft knife
metal ruler
stencil brush
fine artist's paintbrush
PVA (white) glue
pressed pansy flowers and yellow chrysanthemum petals
tweezers
kitchen sponge
water-based matt varnish and brush

1 Paint the tray with two coats of pale blue emulsion (latex) paint and leave to dry. Mark out a grid of squares on the main part of the tray, using a ruler and soft pencil.

2 Trace one of the squares on to thin paper. Place some stencil acetate on top and use a craft knife and metal ruler to cut out the shape so that a square hole is left in the acetate.

3 Place the square stencil on the tray, aligning it with one of the squares on the marked grid. Take up a little yellow paint on a stencil brush, dab off the excess then apply to the tray. Colour all the alternate squares yellow. Leave to dry.

4 Using the same stencil, colour the remaining squares white. Leave to dry.

5 Arrange the flowers and petals on the squares. Move each flower aside in turn and, using a fine paintbrush, apply a little PVA (white) glue on each square.

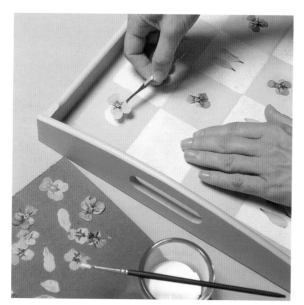

6 Place the flowers or petals carefully on the glue, using tweezers.

7 When the design is complete, press the flowers and petals down gently with a slightly damp sponge and wipe away any excess glue. Leave to dry then apply a coat of varnish.

FLORAL GLASSWARE

Pressed flowers and glass are a particularly successful combination. Here the shapes of different petals echo the contours of a wine glass and a bowl, ideal for floating candles.

YOU WILL NEED
clean, dry wine glass
pressed gerbera petals and pentas flowers
sheet of paper
PVA (white) glue
fine artist's paintbrush
tweezers
kitchen sponge
cotton bud
clear acrylic spray
glass paint
large glass bowl
pressed rose petals

1 For the wine glass: Make sure the glass is free from grease. Place the gerbera petals and pentas flowers face down on a sheet of paper. Apply a little PVA (white) glue on the back with a fine paintbrush. Use the tweezers to position each petal and flower in turn on the side of the glass.

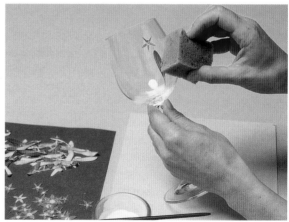

2 Press gently in place with a slightly damp sponge, taking care not to smudge the glue.

3 When the design is complete, remove any surplus glue with a slightly damp cotton bud.

4 Leave to dry then apply a coat of clear acrylic spray.

5 Using a fine paintbrush, decorate the stem of the glass with glass paint. Leave to dry.

Above: Matching water glasses would make an attractive feature for a special occasion.

6 For the glass bowl: Glue the petals and flowers around the outside in the same way. Use a damp sponge to make sure all the edges are stuck down.

7 When the glue is dry, cover the bowl with clear acrylic spray.

TRANSPARENT BOX LID

Transform a plain cardboard box with an acetate window in the lid, decorated with flowers and leaves. Layers of tissue paper give the box a soft, romantic look.

YOU WILL NEED
small cardboard box with lid
pencil
metal ruler
utility knife
cutting mat
white or slightly off-white emulsion (latex) paint
small decorator's paintbrush
handmade tissue paper
PVA (white) glue
medium-sized artist's paintbrush
scissors
clear acetate
pressed flowers and leaves, in predominantly yellow colours
varnish

1 Mark a line all round the lid of the box about 2 cm/³/₄ in from the edge. Using a utility knife and metal ruler, cut out to leave a hole.

2 Paint the box and the lid, including the insides, with white or slightly off-white (emulsion) paint. Apply two coats if necessary.

3 Tear the tissue paper into fairly small pieces. Begin to cover the box and lid with layers of tissue paper pieces, sticking them down with PVA (white) glue. Cover the raw edges of the hole in the lid.

4 Cut a piece of acetate to fit inside the lid. Arrange the pressed flowers and leaves on the acetate then fix each in place with a small blob of glue on the back.

5 Cut a piece of tissue paper the same size as the acetate and fit it inside the lid.

6 Glue the acetate, decorated side down, on top of the tissue paper so that the flowers and leaves are sandwiched between the two. Neaten the edges of the lid with pieces of torn tissue paper glued in place.

7 Glue a few extra flowers and leaves around the sides of the lid and the box. Varnish the box and the lid but not the tissue and acetate panel.

COUNTRY-STYLE NOTICEBOARD

Natural linen and linen tape tone beautifully with the pressed flowers and leaves, and the colour-washed wooden frame in this attractive design.

YOU WILL NEED

large, rectangular, wooden picture frame
medium-sized decorator's paintbrush
off-white emulsion (latex) paint
pressed flowers (e.g. daisies, small white chrysanthemums)
pressed leaves (e.g. senecio and artemisia)
tape measure
PVA (white) glue
fine artist's paintbrush
spray matt acrylic varnish
saw
MDF (medium-density fibre board)
scissors
natural linen or linen-look fabric
staple gun
soft pencil
linen dressmaking tape
hammer
decorative upholstery nails
picture wire or cord for hanging (optional)

1 Paint the picture frame lightly with off-white emulsion (latex) paint so that the texture of the wood shows through. Leave to dry.

2 Plan the arrangement of the flowers and leaves on the frame. Start in the centre of one short side and work outwards, using a tape measure if necessary. Apply a little PVA (white) glue to the back of each flower or leaf and stick in place.

3 When the design is complete and the glue is dry, spray the frame with matt acrylic varnish. Repeat if necessary but take care not to flatten the flowers.

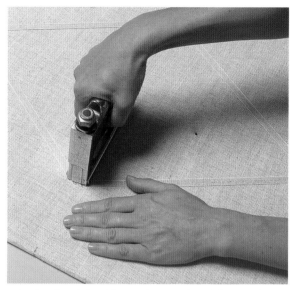

4 Cut a piece of MDF (medium-density fibre board) to fit inside the frame. Cover with linen or linen-look fabric, securing the fabric at the back with a staple gun.

5 On the right side, mark out a large diamond in the centre, using a soft pencil. Cut four lengths of linen tape to fit and lay in place, stapling them together at the corners.

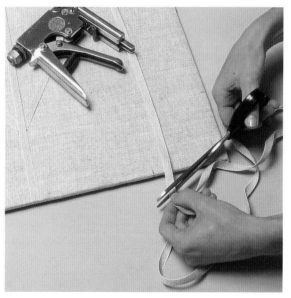

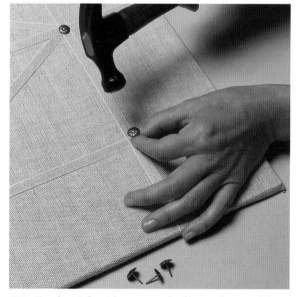

6 Arrange more lines of tape in a pleasing design, weaving them over and under. Trim the ends and secure at the back of the board with the staple gun.

7 On the right side, secure the lines of tape with upholstery nails spaced at regular intervals. Fit the decorated board securely into the frame. Attach picture wire or cord at the top for hanging, if required.

HYDRANGEA GIFT WRAP

This co-ordinated card, parcel and gift tag are simple to make but look very stylish.
The pressed hydrangea flowers are very distinctive.

YOU WILL NEED
scissors
thick cream paper
textured pale lilac paper
metal ruler
PVA (white) glue
fine artist's paintbrush
medium sized artist's paintbrush
large pressed petals
tracing paper
pressed hydrangea flower heads
white layout paper
double-sided tape
cream cotton tape
hole punch
1 cm/ ¹/₂ in wide translucent ribbon

1 For the card: Cut a 15 x 23 cm/ 6 x 9 in rectangle of cream paper and fold in half widthways. Tear a 10 x 13 cm/4 x 5 in rectangle of pale lilac paper, pulling the paper against a metal ruler to give a "deckle" edge.

2 Using PVA (white) glue, attach the lilac paper to the front of the folded cream paper.

3 Using a fine artist's paint-brush, apply a small amount of glue in turn to the back of five large pressed petals. Glue one to each corner of the lilac paper and one in the centre.

4 Tear five small rectangles of tracing paper, each approximately 2.5 x 4 cm/ 1 x 1¹/₂ in. Glue one on top of each petal.

5 Glue four pressed hydrangea flower heads in the spaces between the petals.

6 For the parcel: place the gift in a box. Wrap it in white paper, secured with double-sided tape.

7 Using PVA glue and an artist's paintbrush, glue large petals randomly over the top and long sides of the parcel.

8 Cut a strip of tracing paper to wrap round the parcel, covering the petals, and secure at the bottom of the parcel with double-sided tape. Tie a length of cream tape around the parcel, finishing with a bow.

Above: A parcel this pretty is a gift in itself.

9 For the gift tag: reduce or enlarge the gift tag template at the back of the book and transfer on to thick cream paper. Tear out the shape against a metal ruler. Glue on to a piece of pale lilac paper 5 mm/¼ in larger all round, and tear out as before.

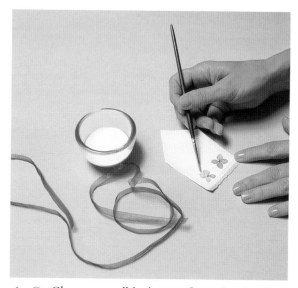

10 Glue two small hydrangea flower heads to the flat end of the gift tag. Punch a hole in the pointed end, and thread a length of translucent ribbon through.

FLOWERY WASTEPAPER BASKET

Make your own basket out of coils of corrugated paper then decorate it with flowers.
Corrugated paper is similar to corrugated cardboard but one side is flat.

YOU WILL NEED
pencil
ruler
corrugated paper
scissors
strong PVA (white) glue and brush
paperclips
white tissue paper
kitchen sponge
pressed montbretia, with stems
dressmaker's pins
pressed flower heads in yellow and orange
spray matt varnish

1 Mark the corrugated paper into eight strips 3 cm x 2 m/1 in x 2 yd, with the flutes running across each strip. Cut out.

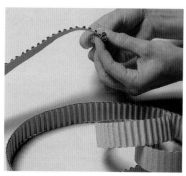

2 To make the base of the basket, spread PVA (white) glue along the centre of one strip and roll up from one end.

3 Take a second strip and tear off 2.5 cm/1 in from one end. Glue the flat surface over the end of the coil, and roll up to complete the base.

4 Join on a third strip in the same way. Begin to shape the sides of the basket by coiling the strips around the base and gluing them in place. Gradually increase the angle so that the strips only cover half of the previous coil.

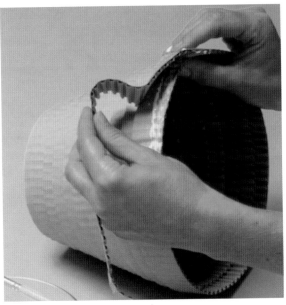

5 Continue building up the sides, joining on extra strips. You can use paperclips to hold the strips in place until the glue is dry.

6 When you reach the last strip, begin to level off the top of the basket.

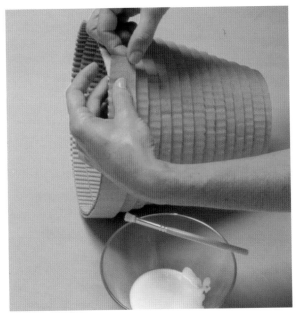

7 Once the top is level, wind the strip round once to create a rim. Tear away the flutes on the reverse of the strip and make a smooth join.

8 Dilute the PVA glue with five times the amount of water. Tear the tissue paper into rough pieces and apply glue on to each piece with a sponge.

9 Cover the basket with overlapping pieces of tissue paper, pressing them down gently with the sponge. The tissue will tighten as it dries.

10 Take each montbretia in turn and spread glue along the back of the petals and the stem. Press on to the side of the basket and hold until dry. Use a pin to hold the end of the stem in position.

11 Arrange the montbretia evenly around the sides of the basket, then fill in the spaces with yellow and orange flower heads.

12 Apply torn strips of tissue paper over the pressed flowers and stems to soften the effect and secure the ends of the stems. Leave to dry, then spray with several coats of matt varnish.

CORNFLOWER HANGING

Place this delicate hanging on the wall, or in a window where the light will filter through the scrim fabric. The fringed edges give an attractive, textural effect.

YOU WILL NEED
ruler
scissors
1.5 m² (1½ yd²) scrim
bodkin
dressmaker's pins
sewing machine
matching sewing thread
pressed cornflowers, with stems
small pressed leaves
PVA (white) glue
fine artist's paintbrush
kitchen sponge
bradawl (awl)
90 cm (36 in) piece of bamboo cane
jute twine

1 Cut an 80 cm x 1 m/30 in x 1 yd rectangle of scrim. Using a bodkin, fray one short side to make a fringe about 10 cm/4 in deep.

2 Cut out twelve 15 cm/6 in squares of scrim. Fray the sides of each square for about 2 cm/³/₄ in.

3 Fold then pin a 2.5 cm/1 in double hem along both long sides of the main scrim rectangle. Using a small zigzag stitch, machine along the inner fold on each side.

4 Fold, pin and stitch a 2.5 cm/1 in double hem along the top edge in the same way. This will be the casing for the bamboo cane.

5 Pin the frayed squares to the main rectangle in four evenly spaced rows of three squares. Zigzag stitch in place around all four edges.

6 Arrange the pressed cornflowers and leaves on the scrim squares to make a pleasing composition.

7 Apply PVA (white) glue to the back of each cornflower and leaf, using a fine paintbrush.

8 Carefully position the cornflowers and leaves on the scrim squares.

9 When the design is complete, gently press each element in place with a slightly damp sponge.

10 Using a bradawl (awl), pierce a small hole at each end of the bamboo cane. Thread the cane through the casing at the top of the hanging.

11 Thread a long length of jute twine through the holes at each end of the bamboo cane and tie together for hanging.

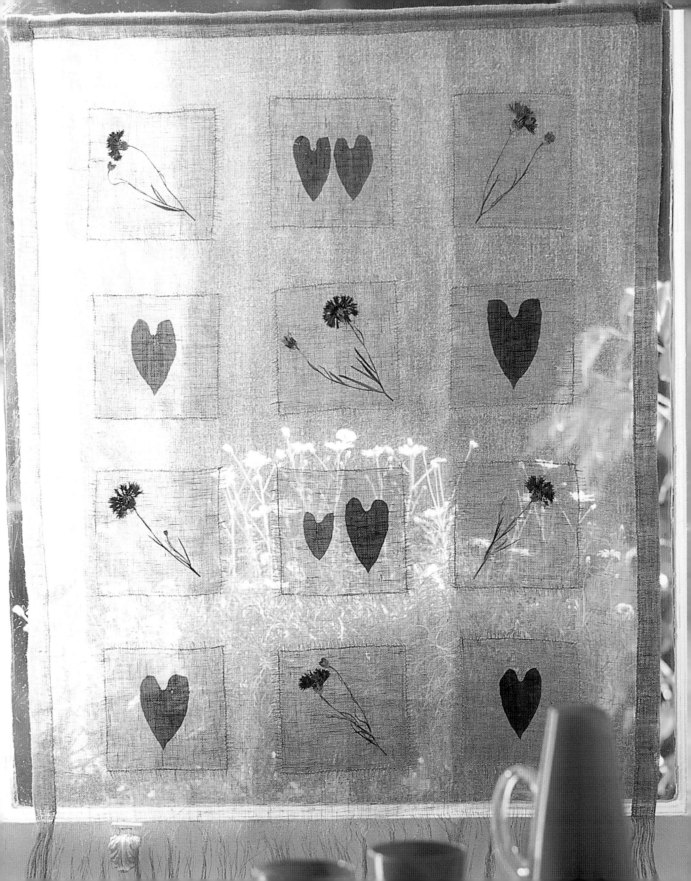

CHRISTMAS ROSE COASTERS

Preserve single, beautiful flower heads in squares of clear resin for a lovely, fresh effect.
Try romantic love-in-a-mist flowers as an alternative.

YOU WILL NEED
scissors
thick card (cardboard)
10 cm/4 in square block of MDF (medium-density fibre board)
masking tape
plastic packing tape
rubber mould-making material
plastic container, for mixing
spoon
clear casting resin
pressed Christmas rose flower heads
dressmaker's pin
fine-grade sandpaper

1 Cut out a card (cardboard) square about 2.5 cm/1 in larger all round than the block of MDF (medium-density fibre board). Cut four card strips to fit along the sides.

2 Attach the card strips to each side of the card square with masking tape.

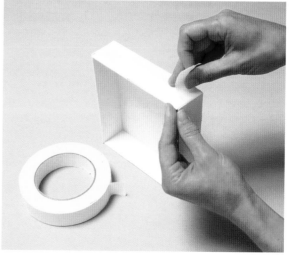

3 Bend up the strips to form a shallow box and secure with masking tape.

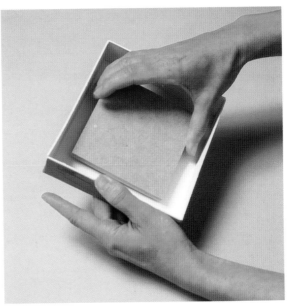

4 Attach strips of packing tape to the outside edges of the box to make it watertight.

5 Place the block of MDF in the centre of the card box.

6 Following the manufacturer's instructions, make up enough rubber mould-making material to fill the box. Pour the solution into the box, then tap the sides gently to remove air bubbles. Leave overnight to set.

7 Carefully remove the rubber mould, including the MDF block, from the box.

8 Turn the mould upside down and prise the MDF block from the centre.

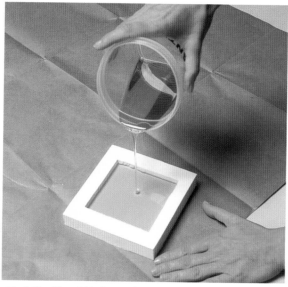

9 Mix 50 ml/2 fl oz of resin solution, according to the manufacturer's instructions. Pour into the mould, filling it to about halfway. Leave to set.

10 Take a pressed Christmas rose flower head and place it face up in the centre of the layer of resin.

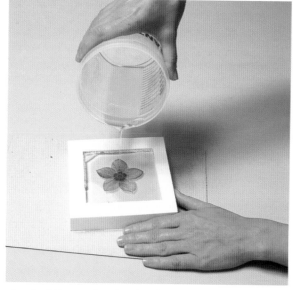

11 Mix another batch of resin as before, and fill the mould, covering the flower head completely. Prick any air bubbles with a pin, then leave for about 24 hours to harden. Remove the resin coaster from the mould, and sand the edges smooth.

MATERIALS

In addition to pressed flowers and leaves, the most important materials to collect are interesting papers of all kinds.

BAMBOO
Green bamboo cane looks attractive once peeled, while mature bamboo is much tougher.

CANDLES
Church candles are high in beeswax and therefore burn slowly.

CASTING RESIN
A clear material used with a mould to make solid objects.

CORRUGATED PAPER
Similar to corrugated cardboard, except that one side is flat.

FABRICS
Tulle, organdie, linen and linen-look fabrics have many uses.

GLUE
Use PVA (white) glue for sticking paper, pressed flowers and leaves.

LAMINATING FILM
A clear iron-on film for use when varnish is inappropriate.

LAVENDER
Hang up to dry completely, then rub off the individual flowers.

LINEN TAPE
Traditional dressmaker's tape looks attractive with natural materials.

MOULD-MAKING MATERIAL
Use rubber or alginate mould-making material with plaster of Paris to create different moulds.

PAINTS
For large areas use emulsion (latex) paint, while for small areas and stencilling use acrylic paint.

PAPERS
For a transparent layer use fine tissue paper, tracing paper or waxed sandwich paper. Make papier-mâché with newspaper, handmade paper or tissue paper.

PRESSED FLOWERS
Prepare a selection of pressed flowers (see Basic Techniques).

STRING
Use natural-coloured string to enhance pressed flower projects.

VARNISH
Seal and protect finished designs with varnish or clear acrylic spray.

Opposite: organdie (1), handmade paper (2), laminating film (3), plaster of paris (4), glue (5), lavender (6), scrim (7), string and linen tape (8), pressed flowers (9), mould-making material (10), paints (11), candle (12), corrugated paper (13)

EQUIPMENT

Apart from a flower press, most of the tools and equipment are commonly used and widely available.

BALL
Use a polystyrene ball to make a round mould.

BRADAWL (AWL)
Used to pierce small holes, in paper or card (cardboard).

DRILL
Use a hand or electric drill, with a suitable-sized drill bit.

FLOWER PRESS
An essential item. Available in craft shops, or you can make your own (see Basic Techniques).

GLUE GUN
Useful if you need to do a lot of accurate gluing.

MASKING TAPE
Used to hold materials together temporarily.

MITRE BLOCK
For sawing accurate angles, such as on the corners of a frame.

PAPER-MAKING FRAME
Two wooden frames are used to make sheets of handmade paper.

SANDPAPER
Sandpaper is used to smooth wood, papier-mâché or resin.

SAUCEPAN
Used with a heatproof bowl to heat candle wax.

SAW
Use a saw to cut wood and MDF (medium-density fibre board).

SCISSORS
Use a strong pair of scissors to cut out card (cardboard) and a smaller pair for intricate paper shapes.

SPONGE
Use a damp sponge to gently press down petals to ensure they are properly adhered to the surface.

STAPLE GUN
Used to fire staples into thick cardboard, wood or fabric.

UTILITY KNIFE
Use with a metal ruler to cut thicker card (cardboard) or board.

Opposite: sandpaper (1), saw (2), mitre block (3), strong scissors (4), utility knife (5), drill (6), hammer (7), bradawl (awl) (8), metal ruler (9), saucepan (10), glue gun (11), staple gun (12), flower press (13), bowl (14), sponge (15), masking tape (16), paintbrushes (17), polystyrene ball (18), paper-making frame (19), needle (20), small scissors (21), tweezers (22)

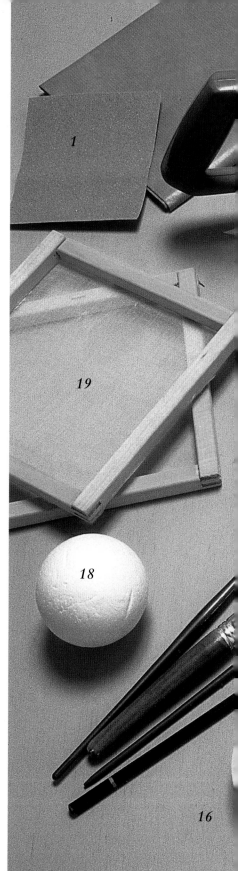

BASIC TECHNIQUES

Always pick flowers and leaves when they are fully open and dry, as any extra moisture will lengthen the pressing process. Here are instructions for preparing, pressing and finishing fresh material, and for making your own flower press.

PREPARING FRESH FLOWERS AND LEAVES FOR PRESSING

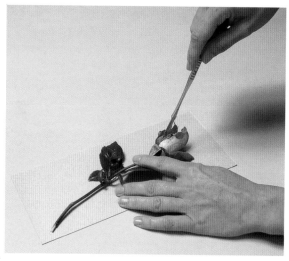

1 Cut bulky flower heads, such as rosebuds, in half, using a craft knife.

2 Reduce the height of a thick calyx by snipping close to the petals with small scissors. Be careful not to snip too closely or the petals may fall out.

3 Pare down thick stems, using a craft knife.

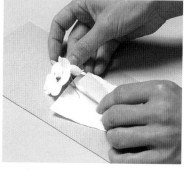

4 To remove excess moisture from a fleshy stem, place in a folded piece of kitchen paper and squeeze with your fingers.

5 You can also run your finger-nail along the stem to remove moisture.

USING A FLOWER PRESS

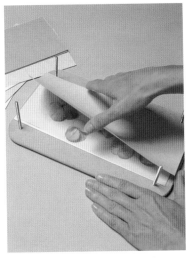

1 Have a pile of blotting paper and card (cardboard) ready to hand. Remove the top of the flower press. Place a sheet of blotting paper in the press, then lay the flowers or leaves face down on top.

2 Place another sheet of blotting paper carefully on top.

3 Continue layering the filled sheets of blotting paper separating each layer with pieces of card.

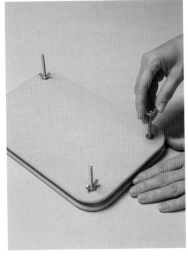

4 Place the top of the flower press in position.

5 Screw the wing nuts down tightly. Leave in a warm, dry place for about six weeks.

6 When the pressed material is completely flat and dry, remove it carefully with tweezers.

PRESSING FLOWERS AND LEAVES

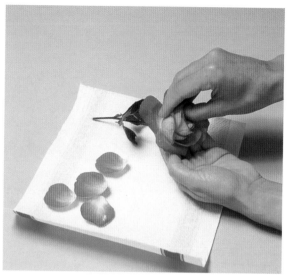

1 The simplest method is to use a book. Lay the flowers or leaves face down on a folded piece of blotting paper and place between the pages of the book. Put a weight on top, and leave in a warm, dry place for about six weeks.

2 To press individual petals, lay them out on a folded piece of blotting paper and press between the pages of a book, as in step 1.

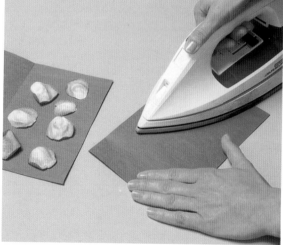

3 A quick method of pressing small flowers, leaves or petals is to iron them. Place them on a folded piece of blotting paper, and iron using a moderate setting.

FINISHING

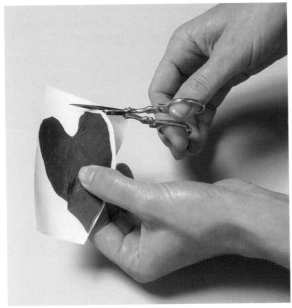

1 Iron-on laminating film can be used to protect pressed flowers and leaves on fabric. Cut a piece of film slightly larger all round than the flower or leaf.

2 Position the flower or leaf on the fabric. Peel the backing paper off the laminating film.

3 Place the laminating film adhesive side down over the flower or leaf.

4 Replace the backing paper, then iron over it to fix the film to the fabric.

5 Spray varnish or clear acrylic is a quick and easy way to seal and protect a finished pressed flower design. Brush-on varnish can be used if there are no loose or delicate elements.

MAKING YOUR OWN FLOWER PRESS

YOU WILL NEED
pencil
two rectangles or squares of MDF
(medium-density fibre board)
masking tape
drill
strong scissors
thick card (cardboard)
blotting paper
four 10 cm/4 in bolts and matching wing nuts and washers

1 Mark the position for a hole in each corner of one of the pieces of MDF (medium-density fibre board). Place the two pieces together and secure with masking tape. Drill holes at each marked point. Cut several pieces of card (cardboard) and blotting paper slightly smaller than the MDF pieces. Cut across the corners as shown.

2 Place the card and blotting paper in the press, with two pieces of blotting paper between each card layer.

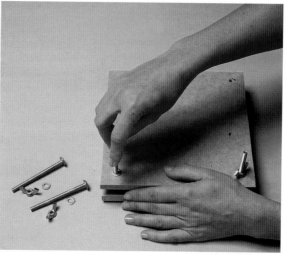

3 Insert the bolts in the drilled holes, then screw on the washers and wing nuts.

TEMPLATES

Either reduce or enlarge the templates on a photocopier to the required size, or trace the design,

and draw a grid of evenly spaced squares over your tracing. Draw a different-sized grid on to

another piece of paper and copy the outline square by square.

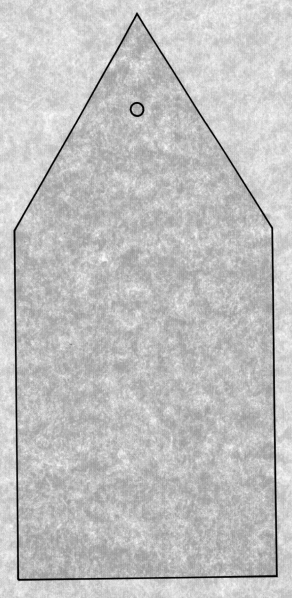

Hydrangea Gift Wrap – gift tag, pp 66–69

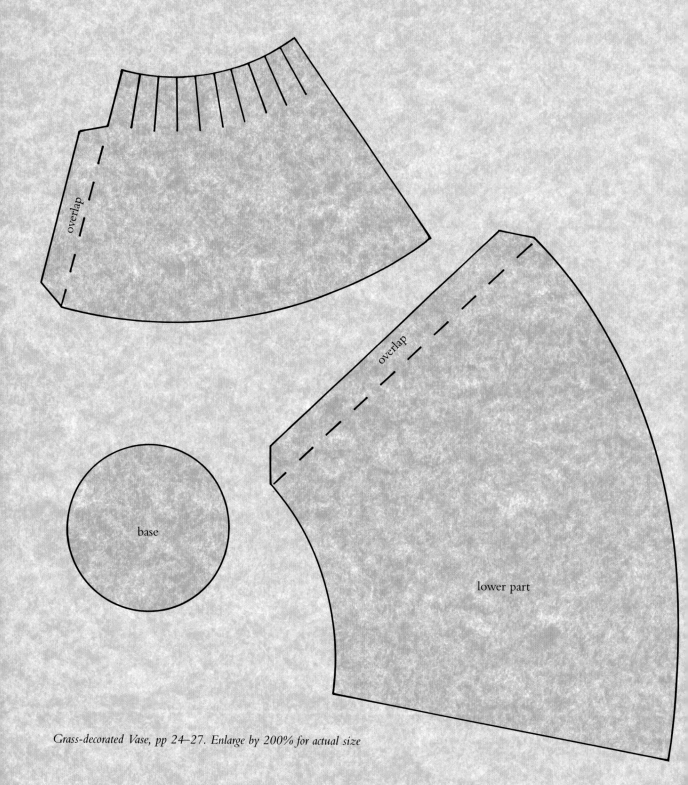

Grass-decorated Vase, pp 24–27. Enlarge by 200% for actual size

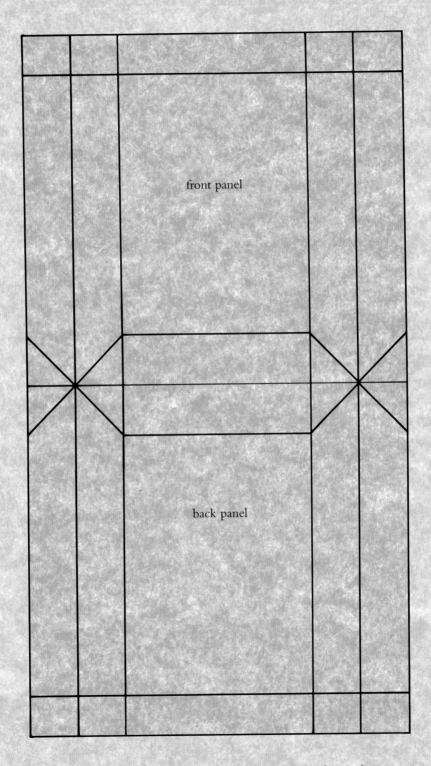

front panel

back panel

Waxed Flower Gift Bags, pp 10–13. Enlarge by 200% for actual size

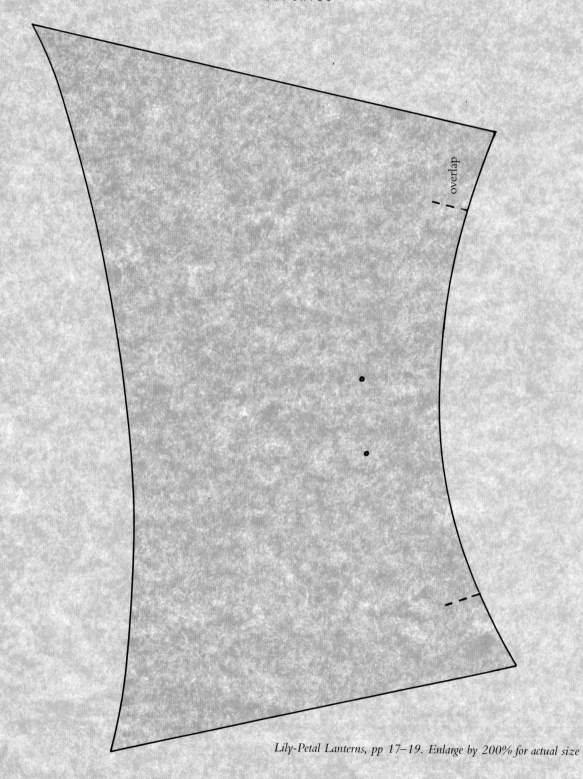

overlap

Lily-Petal Lanterns, pp 17–19. Enlarge by 200% for actual size